Fuel the Body

Eating Well

by Amanda Doering Tourville   illustrated by Ronnie Rooney

PiCTURE WiNDOW BOOKS
Minneapolis, Minnesota

Special thanks to our advisers for their expertise:

Nora L. Howley, M.A., School Health Consultant
Silver Spring, Maryland

Terry Flaherty, Ph.D., Professor of English
Minnesota State University, Mankato

Editor: Christianne Jones
Designer: Tracy Davies
Page Production: Michelle Biedscheid
Art Director: Nathan Gassman
The illustrations in this book were created with
ink and watercolor.

Picture Window Books
151 Good Counsel Drive
P.O. Box 669
Mankato, MN 56002-0669
877-845-8392
www.picturewindowbooks.com

Printed in the United States of America.

All books published by Picture Window Books
are manufactured with paper containing at least
10 percent post-consumer waste.

Library of Congress Cataloging-in-Publication Data
Tourville, Amanda Doering, 1980-
Fuel the body : eating well / by Amanda Doering Tourville ;
illustrated by Ronnie Rooney.
p. cm. — (How to be healthy!)
Includes index.
ISBN 978-1-4048-4814-6 (library binding)
1. Nutrition—Juvenile literature. I. Rooney, Ronnie, ill. II. Title.
RA784.T684 2009
613.2—dc22   2008006420

Eating good food keeps your body healthy. A good diet helps your body stay strong. It also gives you energy. There are many ways to eat well every day.

Kara eats breakfast every morning before school. With a healthy breakfast, Kara knows she will stay full until lunch.

Don't skip breakfast. You will be hungrier later in the day.

At lunch, Kara chooses a grilled chicken sandwich and a salad instead of fried chicken and chips.

For dessert, she has some strawberries.

Fruits and vegetables are very nutritious. You should eat at least three servings of fruit and three servings of vegetables every day.

After school, Kara wants a snack. She eats an apple and some almonds instead of cookies.

Apples and almonds have fiber in them. Fiber makes you feel full.

Kara's dad makes a nutritious dinner.

Kara eats fish, potatoes, carrots, and broccoli. She has a glass of milk with her dinner.

Milk and milk products contain calcium. Calcium helps grow strong bones. Kids should drink milk or eat cheese or yogurt every day.

For dessert, Kara has a small piece of chocolate cake. She eats it slowly and enjoys it. Yum!

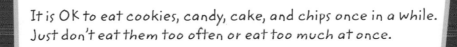

It is OK to eat cookies, candy, cake, and chips once in a while. Just don't eat them too often or eat too much at once.

13

Kara is full, so she stops eating. She doesn't like to feel uncomfortable from eating too much.

When you are full, stop eating. Eating too much can leave you feeling sick.

Kara is hungry for a bedtime snack. She eats a piece of whole-wheat toast with jam and some yogurt.

Whole grains contain fiber, vitamins, and minerals. They help prevent heart disease.

Kara likes burgers and fries but doesn't eat them very often. She knows that fast food has a lot of fat and salt in it.

Fast food is OK for a treat, but you shouldn't eat it very often. Eating too much fat and salt can cause health problems.

At a friend's house, Kara asks for water or juice instead of soda. Soda has too much sugar in it.

It is always best to drink water instead of soda.
Make sure to drink plenty of water every day.

Kara tries to eat a balanced diet based on the food pyramid. She tries to eat the right number of servings of fruits, vegetables, grains, milk, and meat every day.

Kara eats well and stays healthy.

The food pyramid shows you how much you should eat from each food group every day. Visit www.mypyramid.gov for more information.

To Learn More

More Books to Read

Barron, Rex. *Showdown at the Food Pyramid.* New York: G. P. Putnam's Sons, 2004.

Leedy, Loreen. *The Edible Pyramid: Good Eating Every Day.* New York: Holiday House, 2007.

Rockwell, Lizzy. *Good Enough to Eat: A Kid's Guide to Food and Nutrition.* New York: Harper Collins, 1999.

On the Web

FactHound offers a safe, fun way to find Web sites related to topics in this book. All of the sites on FactHound have been researched by our staff.

1. Visit *www.facthound.com*
2. Type in this special code: 1404848142
3. Click on the FETCH IT button.

Your trusty FactHound will fetch the best sites for you!

Look for all of the books in the How to Be Healthy! series:

Brush, Floss, and Rinse: Caring for Your Teeth and Gums
Fuel the Body: Eating Well
Get Up and Go: Being Active
Go Wash Up: Keeping Clean

Index